# Pacemaker

David Toms is a writer from Waterford, now living and working in Norway. His poetry collections include *Northly* (Turas Press, 2019), *Soma | Sema* (Knives Forks and Spoons Press, 2011), and several chapbooks. His creative work has been published in a wide range of magazines and anthologies across Ireland, the UK, the US and Europe, including in several issues of *Banshee*.

# Pacemaker

David Toms

BANSHEE PRESS

First published 2022 by
Banshee Press
www.bansheelit.com

A CIP record for this title is available from the British Library.

Banshee Press gratefully acknowledges
the financial assistance of the Arts Council.

ISBN: 978-1-8383126-5-7

Set in Palatino by Eimear Ryan
Cover design by Anna Morrison
Printed and bound in Great Britain by Clays Ltd, Elcograf S.p.A.

*This is for Miriam*

# Contents

# First Steps

EVERY TIME I WRITE about my heart, I write about walking. Every time I write about walking, I write about my heart.

I AM ONE of a group of people called 'Heart Children' in Ireland. I was born on 19 February 1988 presenting with symptoms in line with transposition of the great arteries, a rare congenital heart defect. Where one in a hundred children are born with a heart defect, a tiny percentage within that are born with transposition of the great arteries. Before they knew what the defect was, people like me used to be called blue babies. Cyanotic is the medical term. Transposition is a heart defect in which the aorta arises from the right ventricle and the pulmonary artery arises from the left ventricle. This switch from the norm causes deoxygenated blood from the right heart to be pumped immediately through the aorta and circulated throughout the body and the heart itself, bypassing the lungs altogether. In this same condition, the left heart continuously pumps oxygenated blood back into the lungs through the pulmonary artery, instead of out into the body's circulation as it normally would. In effect, two separate 'parallel' circulatory systems are created. Two routes. Two trails. When we are born, the deoxygenated blood in our systems turns our skin blue, especially at the extremities, like the nose or fingertips. It wasn't until 1957 that Åke Senning, a Swedish doctor, performed the first successful repair of this condition. In 1963, William Mustard, a Canadian doctor, performed a new procedure that improved on Senning's. Before the innovations of Senning and Mustard, the condition was usually fatal for the newborn.

By the time I was born, the Senning and Mustard procedures, known as atrial switch operations, were practised in Ireland. In 1979, Maurice Neligan – a Dublin surgeon – had perfected the complex surgical technique precluding the need to send cyanotic babies like me to London for treatment. Neligan and another surgeon, Freddie Wood, both spent time in the 1980s at Harefield and Papworth hospitals in the UK, expanding their knowledge of a wide range of congenital heart defects, which they began operating on as early as 1974. Freddie Wood was the lead surgeon on my operation. In 1985 he was part of the team that performed Ireland's first heart transplant. When he operated on me in May 1988, he was in the middle of a long-running and public battle with the Department of Health over delays with procedures for children like me. Cuts to the health budget had brought him into the public eye. By February 1988, 250 children were awaiting life-saving operations in Ireland. I would soon join them.

I TRY TO IMAGINE the fear my mother must have felt seeing my colour change after birth. I was her sixth child and the first born sick. The realization that must have swept over the nurses and doctors. Their ability to act fast. In no time being moved from Airmount to Ardkeen to Crumlin. I was baptized almost immediately, so that my immortal soul might not be endangered should I die. That was the Ireland I was born into. In the maternity ward in Airmount Hospital, as I turned blue, and with my mother exhausted from labour, such things were on the minds of the nurses and doctors. That whatever else, this blue baby need not endure purgatory. I must be named in the eyes of God. Panicking, asked what the boy's name was to be, and knowing it might not matter much since no one might ever call me from the street or playground in years to come – rushed – my mam chose a name, any name. My name.

My mother, Maria, has kept every receipt. *To Our Lady's Hospital for Sick Children, Crumlin 19/2/88–29/2/88. 10 days at £70: £700. Inpatient care: £100. Total: £800.* I was admitted to Crumlin again on 4 May 1988 for the procedure to save my life. I would stay there for sixteen days. *Operation on 9/5/88: £850. Anaesthetist, fees due for professional attendance: Theatre £120. Six nights in intensive care: £120. Total: £240. Received with thanks.*

THAT WAS THE START of it. From then on, every year, usually in the summer months, I would make the trip to Dublin to see Dr Desmond Duff in Crumlin. All of those meetings are a single meshed memory now but his kind demeanour remains in my mind. The chill of his stethoscope, the dark hair on his hands, his knuckles as he rolled the echo Doppler over my chest with the cold jelly while I lay sideways, arm tucked under a pillow, wanting to turn my head towards the screen. The sound of my heart as the roller ball moved over my chest. He had a way of sighing that was a way of speaking. He had an easy manner with me as I progressed from child to surly teenager, too clever – he may have thought – for my own good.

IF YOU SPEND ENOUGH time with me, my heart condition will come up. It's an unavoidable fact of my life and reality. To explain why I can't do something. Or why I don't want to do another. I push against my limits, but I have to avoid crossing a border I can't quite see. I am still learning because the doctors are still learning. Never have so many with our conditions lived past infancy. Our lives as adults remain a mystery. Some things they know. People with transposition, like me, tend to have more complications based on the type of operation they underwent, and these can present challenges later in life. The risk of sudden cardiac death is present, but less likely than it used to be. Medication around the heart is more and more sophisticated, surgical interventions more successful in managing the condition.

In August 2020, I was admitted to hospital for the third time that year. For me, 2020 was marked by recovery and relapse, lockdown and self-isolation. As the world churned, my body churned with it. My third stay was shorter than the first that year. Shorter too than the second. The third I was awake for – aware of everything happening to my body as they operated. It had been delayed for as long as possible, but the time had come for further surgery. A new pace was being set. The first steps of a new life.

A PACEMAKER, meaning the one who sets the pace of a race, was a term first coined in the 1880s. An early example of its usage comes from *The Pall Mall Gazette* in 1884. In 1958 two Swedish surgeons – one of them Åke Senning – implanted the first electronic pacemaker with a rechargeable nickel-cadmium battery into the chest of a forty-year-old patient. It helped to regulate the pace of his heart. Blood is pumped from our hearts out and around the network of vessels that stretch for thousands of miles. We say it is pumped, that it courses through our veins. The coursing of blood in its oldest sense is a transitive verb – chase, pursue, run after. Intransitive, in Shakespeare's hands, it passed through the natural gates and alleys of the body, swift quicksilver. Our blood flows, courses, from the chambers of the heart – the innermost rooms, private interior, secret portion. Enclosed cavity, these quarters – engine rooms conducting the course of the day. Perhaps, though, it makes more sense to think of our blood walking through our bodies across those thousands of miles. Blood is pumped from the heart around the body at a speed of between three and four miles per hour. The average person walks at the same pace. Blood and feet synchronized as we walk streets, paths, trails, first steps to last.

Crutch

AT ITS EDGES, the forest floor is a green bed of moss and the sun bursting down. It is early September. I am walking in the woods near my new home, about an hour north of Oslo. Into the woods. Through them. Across them. Becoming part of them. Zigzagging up and down between rocks and rotten tree stumps. I spot mushrooms and thick bushes of blueberries. On some rocks, standing alone, there is moss like thickset hair, springy to the touch and knotted in a network of life. I poke my walking stick in front of me to judge the softness of the ground as I move forward, unsure of my footing. I place it on an old moss-covered tree stump, and the bottom of my stick goes straight through the marshy bark, silently. I strafe this way and that. The top of my walking stick glued to my hand with sweat. Who hath not one horse may on a staff ride.

I LIKE MY WALKING sticks to be about shoulder height. It gives more to lean into going up and coming down. With each walk of the woods, I pick up sticks and test them. Walk with them a while to see how they feel in my hand. Gauge the grip. A kind of communion with the dead. Bark hard and dry, knots smoothed only by sanding. It takes weeks. Patient waiting. The drying process. The removal of the bark. It is best to do in springtime when bark has not yet dried in and a stick is easily shorn. Then you must treat the wood. Resurrection is a process.

I PICK THE WALKING stick up early on my walk, spotting it among some felled trees. I turn it over in my hands, gripping my palm against the bark to see how it feels. It seems sturdy and just the right thickness. Not brittle like some branches I try first. It is serviceable for this trip so I begin using it immediately. As I walk here and there through the woods close to the Solar Observatory, I think about what it means to call it my stick. When does a walking stick taken from the forest floor become yours? Does it ever become yours? Why imbue this dead piece of wood with meaning? To what end? To give life back to it? To extend your own inner life out to one more object that contains a piece of you?

WALKING STICKS CONTAIN a kind of power. People put themselves into their walking sticks. They shadow their walks. The way some people seem to swagger with them, loosely held but controlled, pendular-swing in time with their step. As a child, I considered them a sign of infirmity. I couldn't understand why a person who was fit and healthy would want or need what I thought of only as a kind of crutch. Walking sticks were not then fashion items to me. Nor something for the fit walker who wants to walk farther, more expansively – through forests, say, or up a steep hill. When I think of walking sticks, I imagine the deep knottiness of a blackthorn stick. I have always loved the look of the blackthorn. Stick is signified thus for me. I can't think of them without remembering a song I once heard sung by a Scottish singer at the Singers' Club in An Spailpín Fánach in Cork: *A switch of blackthorn I held in my fist / And round his big body I made it to twist / The blood from his napper I quickly did draw / And paid him stock and interest for Erin Go Bragh.*

THERE IS ALSO a vague memory of a blackthorn stick that my dad had for a while, which he kept in our garage. *Cut a stout blackthorn to banish ghost and goblin.* And of the walking sticks in my aunt Breda's house, in the corner of the hallway. I remember running my hands over the knots and the smooth top, fascinated. Walking sticks are close cousins to the wizard's staff in my mind. Gandalf. Merlin. I wonder did Sweeney Peregrine have a stick or a staff on his wanderings.

WE TRANSFER MEANING to things. By itself, this stick was the branch of a chopped-down tree. In my hands, it is a weapon of defence and attack, a portal to a world of wizards. Once a part of the forest, now guiding me through the same place from which it came. The walking staff comes out of the Book of Exodus to us. Moses had one. In Old English it was a stæb. A stave. Staff. Isaiah prophesized that the staff of the mighty would be broken and the earth would be at peace. In the grip of the church it became a bishop's crozier.

In the Schools' Collection of the National Folklore Collection, a story recorded by a pupil in Doolough, County Clare, suggests that no one would make walking sticks from whitethorn. This is because Christ's crown of thorns was said to be from that tree. No one in the district would cut a lone whitethorn because it was said that the tree would be in your bed that night. The berries were understood to be drops of blood. A switch of blackthorn is better for wrapping around the bodies of your enemies anyway.

IN A VIDEO ONLINE, a man named Huw Edwards suggests that to bolster your walking stick, a ram's horn should be boiled in a pot of water for about two hours. Then, it can be taken out and twisted while hot into any shape required. This head can then be fitted to a hazel stick and secured with glue. In this way, Edwards says, a very good walking stick is made.

My walking stick is plain and strong. It guides me between the pines, across the mossy floor of the forest. I rest it against the same rocks where I do. To let a walking stick fall when setting out on a journey is believed to foretell disappointment. Men have made whole trees their walking sticks to fend off giants. They have walked the land to talk to the King of Leinster, cheating death with branches shorn of twigs that took them across their country. Over land and mountain, through hedge and thicket, forest, bramble and briars.

HERMES, MERCURIAL, WALKED with caduceus. Shepherds tend flocks with a crooked walking stick. Sometimes as I walk the woods near Harestua I hear the clanking of a bell around a sheep's neck. I have never seen a shepherd but they are safely ensconced in the forest and its paths. I have walked manmade paths and I have walked those beaten by the sheep. I have walked paths that I alone have created. Made topographies of my own. I have done this with the help of a walking stick I took from the forest floor.

An OLD RIDDLE from County Monaghan asks:

*What still moves when it is dead?*
*A walking stick.*

SOME PEOPLE TAKE DOWN a tree to make a walking stick. Deciduous are best. Sturdy and strong, their bark is hard, not wet like evergreens. You can use ash. Here in Norway, Ash was the first man. Ash and Elm; Adam and Eve. Two trees given life. Then from the throng did three come forth, from the home of the gods, the mighty and gracious; two without fate on the land they found, Ask and Embla, empty of might. Soul they had not, sense they had not, heat nor motion, nor goodly hue; Soul gave Odin, sense gave Hönir, heat gave Lothur and goodly hue. Yggdrasil, the world's tree, was made of ash. It reached the heavens and the depths. The oars of the Vikings. The spears of Odin and Thor. Healer and aid, ash trees are important. Hurl in the hand. Setanta and the hound. Gandalf walked in Tolkien's world with an ash stick. *Der Berggeist*. He could easily have been Krkonoš. As my feet drift in one direction, my mind drifts in another. Drifting feet and mind have their anchor, arm's length and shoulder height ahead.

# Abstract

As a teenager – just after my Junior Certificate – I decided I wanted to understand my heart condition properly. I was tired of feeling my own ignorance when the doctors talked to me about my condition, or when the letters came each year to our house after my consultations. I had a studied aversion to science in secondary school. Thinking myself bookish, I internalized the idea that to be artistically inclined was incompatible with being scientific. I had not yet learned what William James understood a hundred years earlier: that every intellectual option was fraught with risk, and there was no power in the universe, religious or scientific, that could save us from believing too little or too much. I took no science subjects after my Junior Certificate. But with terms flying past me in the doctor's office and at the hospital during my annual checkups, and realizing slowly (too slowly) that my condition was permanent, I decided I wanted to absorb the medical language of the heart. Infarction, aorta, tricuspid, regurgitation, stenosis. Words as full of magic as those of foreign languages, incantatory and separate from my understanding of the world. To command the language of the heart, of my condition, was in some way to command the disease and its hold on my life. To know that I had the Mustard operation at eleven weeks – the procedure employs a baffle to redirect caval blood flow to the left atrium which then pumps blood to the left ventricle which

33

then pumps the deoxygenated blood to the lungs. In a normal heart, deoxygenated blood is pumped into the lungs via the right ventricle. Then it is distributed throughout the body via the left ventricle. In the Mustard procedure, blood is pumped to the lungs via the left ventricle and disseminated throughout the body via the right ventricle. It took me a long time to understand what this meant. That my blood flows differently.

I REMEMBER SITTING in Mr Whittle's English class when we were first introduced to the idea of different registers in language. When he explained the concept, I understood it instinctively. I had witnessed it when I went to the hospital for my annual checkups. The register in which doctors spoke among themselves about my heart was different from the register in which they spoke to my parents about it, or to me. I had learned to navigate those subtle differences since childhood. Before I learned to speak this language myself, I trained my ears to listen for a sign that all is not as well as it first sounds. The slightest inflections that indicate worry. Something being said without being stated. It was the second language I learned, though I didn't realize it then. It was a way to own my illness. To wrest back control. It is alarming to be controlled by something you don't have the means to interrogate. It was another form of literacy, to turn those meaningless, frightening words from abstract descriptions of my heart into a methodology for living. I put my effort into learning this language – it became my second tongue.

I HAVE SPENT a lifetime trying to clarify all of this to people I meet. The emotional and the medical. I have tried to write about it often. One method I had of writing about or around it was poetry. To write a poetry of the heart that understood it not as symbol but as muscle. Talking about it demands highly technical language, a different language of the heart. The heart as muscle, as viscera, seems unrelated to the heart as symbol. I cannot reconcile the heart of literature and love song with the muscle in my chest cavity. We talk so often of broken hearts, mended hearts, the rags of a heart, hearts of gold, glass and stone. We are heartsick, heavy-hearted. Hearts melt and want what they want. We will know in our heart of hearts. We should follow our hearts, we are told. If I follow my heart, with its leaking valves and septal defects, its strange flow through my body, where will I go?

# Method

.

I WAS BORN with a broken heart. A heart too weak for this world. Trans / position of the great arteries. Mustard Senning operation. Captopril. Holter monitors. MRI. Blood pressure. Beta blockers. VO2 max tests. For years I could not connect Dublin in my head. There was the hospital and the waiting room with the fading plastic toys that looked old even when I was little. Our Lady's Hospital for Sick Children, Crumlin. Grafton Street comes into view. Trips with my mother to Marks & Spencer. Being bought off with a trip to McDonald's. There was no Luas then. As I got older, it became the Mater Misericordiae on Eccles Street. Walking up O'Connell Street, beyond Parnell, the Garden of Remembrance, Dorset Street Upper. Later in Oslo, the walk down from Dagaliveien, past Ris kirke to Rikshospitalet. The McDonald's nearby. I would go there after checkups to cheer myself up. To remember the annual trip to Dublin. Fixed in the calendar. Steady points of reference, a through line. Pace. Maker. An engine pumping furiously. Against the tide. Against time. I am my body. Congenital heart disease – or is it defect? It depends on whom you ask. Whichever term of endearment / endangering (what's the difference?), use whichever you prefer.

THE BORDER I LIVE within is my body, the boundary walls my heart. My arms only reach so far. My body stretches only so high. No trespassing beyond this point. Take one twice daily. *Transpose*: a permutation which exchanges two elements and keeps all others fixed. To put it plainly, 'TGA is characterized by ventriculo-arterial discordance: the LV gives rise to the PA, and the RV to the aorta.' This means little enough to me. The dissonance between the physical and that which is invisible becomes a collection of notes moving up or down in pitch by a constant number of semitones. Call it what you will, determinant or detriment, this cause of tears, grief, fears.

ONE DAY I WON'T complete my course. Ramipril (10mg) Digoxin (0,25mg). Entresto. Emconcor. Bisoprolol. My name. My address. However often it changes. As sure as the sun comes up, I cup my hands with water with two pills on my tongue and go. Another day. Each year, I tilt my head to read the records of ECGs: these secret asemic lines, my heart in and on a page. Sometimes I imagine it as music, staccato, uneven steps uphill, across the wide open wild through narrow streets.

Patient Biography

PATIENT: ROOTED IN SUFFERING. *Biography*: the writing of a life. The life written on the body. Scars and dents. The open memory of the whole. To be born with a congenital heart defect is no longer a death sentence. We are living longer and longer. According to at least one study, there is a tendency in adolescents and young adults with congenital heart defects to have unrealistic expectations of longevity. We expect to live only four years less than the general population. While the medical profession is naturally concerned with managing expectations among those of us with congenital heart defects, how we live will matter more than how long we live. A sick person doesn't want to be seen only as a patient. We must be allowed to say that we have a condition, but we are not our condition.

I SPEND A LOT of my life trying to separate out things that are a result of my illness from things that affect anyone. Am I tired because people with my condition get tired more easily, or am I tired because anyone would be tired living as I am? Should I have a beer? Should I switch permanently to low-cholesterol spreads instead of butter? Should I give up red meat? How should I live? Each tiny question is another means of posing the same question over and over: what is it to live with a chronic illness from birth? To live, being reminded every morning that you are only tablets away from death? Learning death's inevitability from a young age. Turn the tap. Cup your hands. Swallow.

THE FIRST SERIOUS DISCUSSIONS I had about death and dying were when I was a teenager in Dr Duff's office at Our Lady's Hospital. The seriousness of my condition slowly dawned on me. Coming out of childhood and its protective cloud into the reality of tricuspid regurgitation, enlarged chambers, a leaking aorta, was frightening. I had no idea how much longer I might live. I wasn't in any immediate and obvious danger, but being a teenager is hard enough without being a sick teenager. Being sick with a congenital heart defect even more difficult because no one can see it. I have all this energy to burn but I tire out so quickly. I can't engage in high-impact cardiovascular exercise because it might cause me to drop dead in the middle of a football pitch.

MY LIFE WAS FULL of football and full of the absence of playing it. I was offered golf as an option. I tried to play it briefly – games of pitch and putt, even getting a little set of left-handed clubs – but it wasn't what I wanted to do. As a child, all I wanted was to play football. I wanted to be a hero like Packie Bonner at Italia '90. I wanted to have the same kind of water bottle he had. The same goalie gloves. I loved getting new jerseys at the start of the season. The smell of a newly bought football from Lifestyle Sports. My dad showing me how to run Vaseline between the stitching to keep the ball in good condition. To make it last longer. I moved from wanting to be Packie Bonner to aspiring to be a midfield general like Roy Keane. To be tough, to show the world I was tough. Determined. That whatever kind of heart problem I had didn't matter. Football was what my brother played, what my dad played, my brothers-in-law. It's what we watched most often as a family together in the evenings and at the weekends – I can hardly remember a time before we had Sky Sports in our house. Childhood and teenage weekends are imprinted with the smell of sideline, wet grass, and dressing room, watching my dad referee local matches or managing his local pub team in the Waterford Pubs League. I grew up hearing about how skilled my dad was at football. Every man we seemed to meet in town slipped me fivers and asked me who I was going to play for and was I going to be as good as him. For a little while, I did summer camps with Bohemians in Waterford and appeared occasionally as a sub. But it was clear I wasn't going to be able to play like the rest of the kids. There were days spent down at Villa's grounds and afterwards in The Munster, eating bacon fries and drinking glasses of free diluted raspberry. Indoor

48

football during PE. The Big Green near my house where we played football all summer, matches lasting what seemed like hours. World Cup. Keepy-uppy. Skills. First to twenty. Stick goalie. Fly keeper. Football was threaded through my teenage years. Waterford United. Friday night down sports centre, the RSC. I went for the first time since I was a kid when Waterford got back into the Premier Division in 2003. The temporary stands behind the goals with my brother John, the late evening summer sun obscuring the view. Then with friends from school. Chips hot with curry burning the roof of your mouth in the cold autumn air at the end of the season. We talked more than we watched the action on the pitch. When it came to picking a Leaving Certificate project, I wrote about the history of football in Waterford. I turned the thing I couldn't play into something else. Something I could read and learn and write about. I became a spectator of the game. I learned how to read it anew. It felt like taking control.

READING AND WRITING BECAME my sports. I learned to play guitar, badly, and I walked and walked in the evenings, writing poems out of the things I saw. From the age of sixteen onwards, I couldn't stop reading. I went on travels with Charley, with Laurie Lee in Spain, Orwell in Paris. I escaped. I wrote terrible poem after terrible poem until they almost became good. In that world, I wasn't limited by cardiologists, by my heart, the speed I could run or walk, or by weight. I was unbounded.

No one – except my family – saw how tired I got. But I knew how tired I could get. Tiredness was a part of my life. I didn't look ill. To the outside world I was your average, slightly chubby, awkward and bookish teenager. Inside, though, my heart could feel like a hammer banging through a wall. People messed with me, tricked me into thinking I'd taken drugs, because I was naive and had to forswear so much of the experimentation of being a teenager. I was forever on the edge of company. Sidelined. Spectator more than participant. I was nervous and anxious around girls I liked because my heart thumped as though it would burst out of my chest.

EXPLAINING MYSELF TO EVERY new person I met was exhausting. I decided to only let some people in. I became cagey. I gauged whether it is worth revealing this truth about myself. I made people uncomfortable with my invisible reality. Forced to confess this secret over and over again when someone says, 'ah go on'. When I moved to Cork in 2006 to study at UCC I couldn't wait to leave behind who I had been in secondary school. Here, I could be whoever I wanted to be. It didn't matter that I hadn't played soccer. Hadn't any medals or trophies. I got here because of my love of books. I kept my condition hidden from people as often and for as long as possible. The experience of college is so much about self-exploration, opening up, but the last thing I wanted to do was tell people – who turned out in the end to be passing acquaintances – the most intimate thing there is to know about me. Nothing kills the mood with a romantic partner quite like having to say, hey look, if I start breathing heavily or get a chesty cough, it's just my heart, okay, but don't worry, I've got it under control. In college, like lots of people, I wanted to pretend I was someone else for a while.

WHEN I WAS YOUNGER, whenever I imagined having sex, I imagined my heart racing too fast and killing me. I knew as little about what sex would do to my heart as I did about how to talk to girls. While other boys my age began boasting about their sexual adventures, I remained sheepish and quiet. I was slow to initiate things with girls I liked. I was afraid of being repulsive. It took me a long time to gain the confidence to start going out with people. I met Miriam at the end of a summer where I had come out of a serious relationship that ended after six years. We swiped right. My opening gambit to her was about the dog she had in her profile picture. It wasn't hers, I found out soon enough. On our first date, she was fifteen minutes late because she'd been distracted by a cat. She showed me photos. When we decided to meet again, I didn't wait very long to tell her about my illness. Having just come out of one relationship, I knew I would have to be upfront if I was starting another. I didn't want to waste her time or mine. I figure if I am asking someone to be with me, they should know what they are letting themselves in for. It seemed amazing to me that Miriam was not fazed by my confession. She just accepted it. I burned with the same sense of shame I'd had as a child as I told her. It was our third date, in a restaurant not far from my apartment, at Náměstí Míru in Prague.

THERE WAS NEVER ANY guarantee that I could work. When I was sixteen, my family helped me to apply for disability allowance. The very phrase is demeaning to me. You are permitted, you are allowed, to be disabled. It means that others are not. It is decided by committee. In a little room in a hotel on the quays in Waterford, some civil servants heard my case and other young people's to determine why we were deserving of being classified as disabled. It wasn't about the money itself but about the security of knowing that I was entitled to it if my health took an unexpectedly negative turn. I had to make my case that I really was as sick as I claimed. I remember the burning sensation in my chest that day. I still remember it. I got the free travel pass that people on disability allowance get. Once, a bus driver questioned my right to have it, because as far as he could see there was nothing wrong with me. The combined weight of humiliations exerts extraordinary pressure.

MY SPEECH WASN'T IMPAIRED; I had no strange gait, no limbs at odd angles. I didn't look disabled, in other words. But I was, and am. The continuous stigmatization of disability has led me at times to disown my own reality. Easier by far to pretend to be just like anyone else. I had all my faculties about me but here I had, inside a little plastic slip, a bit of white and red paper with a photo ID that said to the transport workers of Ireland: *I am disabled*. Still, there were many who were suspicious of a healthy young man presenting with this travel pass. I must have been trying to game the system. I argued once with a driver switching over in Limerick en route to Galway that no one would want to pretend to be disabled just for a free bus ride.

WHAT WAS I SUPPOSED to do? Show everyone the trace of the scar that runs down my chest? The scars where the tubes went into my belly when I was a baby, perhaps? Is that proof enough? The uneven growth of my chest hair because they have to shave it when putting electrodes to my chest in the hospital? My right nostril, a different shape and size from my left, because of the test tube that spent so long resident there when I was born? Why is the burden of proof on me? What makes us so suspicious of others' sickness? Is it fear? Does our existence provide unwelcome reminders to healthy people of their own fragility? Are we spectres among the living, walking *memento mori*?

To have an invisible illness is to invite suspicion. I sometimes felt as though I should keep copies of my medical history on me to throw in the face of those who didn't believe me. I could have it perfect bound, like a dossier, to drop on tables. A book of evidence.

IT IS WRONG to describe it as invisible. It is interior. It is no figment of my imagination. It obscures itself, revealed only occasionally through tiredness, heavy breathing.

ILLNESS INVITES INTROSPECTION. My mind is restless, it wanders unaided. It circles back like a loop walk in Crough Wood. Nøkkelvann. The gap walk in the Nire Valley. Hundtjern-rundet. I am forced to consider constantly the link between body and self. Am I my illness? Is my illness me? Boundaries and definitions shift endlessly. I crossed from Czechia into Poland and Germany in the same looping walk one day. The fixity of such areas is finite. Fleeting. To understand yourself as corporeal entity, to know the limits of your muscles. To appreciate the limitations it places on living unencumbered.

At heart I am a pedestrian. The negative sense of pedestrian as dull, boring and uninspired has been with us since the early 18th century. The idea of the pedestrian as one who walks or prefers to travel on foot, reaches back only to the 17th century. The change came quickly. But walking slows things down. Walking is something that provides many things to me. Time alone. Time to think. Exercise. Exorcise.

BEFORE MY TEENS, I only ever walked with a limited goal in mind: to get to school, say. To the shop. To meet friends up on the big field to kick a ball around. At fifteen, I discovered the joy of walking for its own sake. Of walking by myself. I learned to enjoy the continuous motion. I had nowhere else to put all that energy. From our house in along the Cork Road, sometimes up the High Path, more often in along by Poleberry, John Street, Barronstrand Street, Broad Street, the Quay, by the Mall and Parnell Street. A looping walk. I can taste the cold air of a walk along Barrack Street one Good Friday, past my aunt's house and down into town. The walks in and out to Waterford IT for music lessons in the evening. Guitar on my back. Discman in my pocket. Willy Mason. Bob Dylan. I've been walking ever since.

THERE IS MORE than one way to walk. Slowly. Briskly. We ramble, rove, and roam, we meander, we wander. We take constitutionals. Hike. Stroll. Parade. Swagger. Promenade. Saunter. Troubled, a person might pace a room. Each of these words gives us a way to talk about how we walk that fits the mood and the purpose of walking. I pace the living room with a book in my hands sometimes. The act of walking and thinking, melded, melting. We walk through landscapes for the first time, and every time after in memory and imagination.

Music, songs and poems traverse landscapes real and imagined. 'O'Neill's March'. *As I went out walking one fine summer's morning.* Our highwaymen repair to the mountains with a hundred pounds upon their heads. We go down by the sally gardens. *She moved through the fair.* Floating while walking. Exalted and exultant. We have our pilgrims and their paths. Saint Declan and his well. Our own camino. We are full to the brim of wanderlust, from Mad Sweeney and his peregrinations, to Leopold Bloom and his circumambulations of the city.

I GO WALKING SEVERAL times a day. Morning and evening. I like to walk on the edges of the day. Just before the sun is up, or before it draws down over the horizon. To smell dinners coming from houses. The wood stoves lighting in the winter air. Cool and crisp, smokey. Even on days when I'm feeling unable for it – when it would be easier not to – I drag myself to go out for even ten, fifteen minutes. I have often turned around and come home feeling defeated. Sometimes I push on. Alec Finlay has written in his book *Gathering* about walking and the power of language. How we can invoke the names of places to take mental walks. He reminds his readers that not finishing a walk is as good as finishing one. Distance, incline, length of time travelled don't add up to a good walk. What matters is the pleasure you get from it. The walk from my family home to the local shop on a Saturday for the newspaper is like a small pilgrimage undertaken whenever I am in Waterford. The way it wends past Paddy Brown's pub, crossing at the garage, past what used to be an Xtra-vision, and into a shop that will always be Pat's, no matter the name above the door. A walk I can take anytime I set my mind to it – this little route I walked as a child, a teenager, student, adult; when I lived in Cork, Prague, Oslo. I need only the names of the places I pass through, a little conjuring trick inside the words and all they contain: Sunrise Crescent, Larchville, Lismore Park, and I am walking that way again.

A GOOD WALK CAN be short or long. Ten minutes or ten hours. A walk for the newspaper can be rich with memory and meaning. In the woods, a walk that is focused on picking berries and mushrooms, or staring at a tree, or a brook, or reading a book in the wild, is as good as the walk that took a day and covered forty kilometres. Sometimes, it is better. Many times, more memorable. It beats a path across the hippocampus.

SOMETIMES IN THE MIDDLE of a walk, I forget my forsaking body completely. Walking, my heart is not a weighted stone but light, air-filled. Blood flow and feet entwine; what is hard becomes effortless, joyous. A kind of ecstasy.

EVERY TIME I WRITE about my heart, I write about walking. Every time I write about walking, I write about my heart.

Access

With a full backpack, I took off one afternoon from the apartment Miriam and I had when we first got to Norway: the basement of her mother's house, which had been converted. I headed north along part of what was the old King's Road that stretches from Oslo to Bergen. Down rutted mud tracks I met people on horseback and, turning uphill, my trail took me across a farmer's field. Suddenly my stride was tentative. Unsure. An Irish upbringing led me to fear trespassing. My nervousness about the act of transgression increased as, climbing the hill step by step, the bent bodies of a family harvesting in the field emerged on my right over a low hedge, their voices carrying. One of them, a woman, regarded me briefly before returning to her work. I felt a quickening of my breath, an anxious expectation of admonishment. The indifference was equally baffling. Back at ours, hours later, you reminded me of *allemannsretten* – the right to roam, the right to access. The side of the sign that says nothing. The side made for you and me. Here I can pick berries or mushrooms on the land because it's mine and not mine. Often when I walk, and usually no one else is listening, I sing the chorus of 'The Manchester Rambler'. A reminder that the right I enjoy is not to be taken for granted. The words rise up in me whether deep in Norwegian wood or along the Doneraile in Tramore, stretching my legs out across the sand of Bainbridge Island.

ACCESS IS THE THING. Reading opens paths like those our feet follow, wending our way along a riverbank, a sheep trail, a back road. On days when I'm too tired or too sick to walk, I can retrace walks with words. Can feel again my step, the squelch of my shoe in mud, the wind on my face, the rain seeping through my jacket, the excitement of spotting chanterelles, cloudberries, *krekling* or *tittebær*. I can read a map and imagine the trail, savour the placenames, toss the words around in my mouth and almost vocalize them, see the bodies of water, hear the river moving, feel the biting cold, the warming sun, the wind.

WALKING TAKES ME OUTSIDE my home, my office, myself. Outside my cares. Out beyond my heart to my rotating legs and swinging arms. When I am outside for long enough, outside is no longer the transition space between points A and B: it is the place we are, even as it shifts about us, as we pass through, over and among it. A first walk on a new path seems longer, but with each repetition of the trail, the distance between landmarks that you collect in your mind seems to shorten until the walk becomes a known pleasure, where things are rarely out of place. Walking has a monotonous quality that is part of the appeal of being a pedestrian. This repetitive action, of one foot forward then the other, brings a comfort. You forget you are telling your body to do it; it is borne up from memory. I worry often about when I will take my last breath, my last words. Our first words, first steps are remembered well, but what of our final steps? What would your last walk be?

EVEN WHEN I'M RESTRICTED, with words I have access. That is everyone's right.

AT TABLES, desks, armrests, rocks, I have signed my name, written poems, started essays and articles. Any flat surface will do. With a pen, I have cooked food for family, friends, partners and myself. I have worked and played. I have attended meetings, been in company and alone. I have recorded times, places, dates, and marked events. I have walked and run and stood with a pen in my pocket. I have taught and learned. I've sat still and written furiously. I've sat still and written nothing with the pen limp in my hand. I've been to lakes, on hillsides, and roamed through forests. Up and down streets and across bridges brimful of tourists and tat. I have scribbled and scrawled, drawn and coloured in. I've used pens to pay attention and to distract myself. Idled and organized. Added up and hunkered down. Spelled and misspelled. Given and taken directions. Solved puzzles and come unstuck at crosswords. Pens have been my crutch, walking aid, wayfinder.

Guestbook

ALL ACROSS NORWAY, inside dark green boxes nailed to wooden posts, there are guestbooks to sign. They are found along paths that wind through the woods at common turning points and popular viewing spots; or in the case of mountains, often at the very top. They are usually kept in plastic Ziploc bags inside the postboxes to keep them dry, as they are out all year, whatever the weather. Writing your name in a little guestbook on the side of a woodland path in sub-zero snowy weather is quite the test of your fingers. I never miss a chance to sign one. I often wonder where they go once they are filled up, these hundreds, probably thousands of guestbooks that are kept on trails all over Norway. I usually add my name, and often my dog's name too. Most people don't leave a message, but sometimes record the temperature. Guestbooks are a big thing here: it is common for people to keep one at their *hytte*. The Norwegian Trekking Association also have guestbooks at their various cabins, for those who want to go on long hikes and have a place to stay to break up their journeys overnight. Guestbooks appeal to my sense of posterity. I've signed guestbooks at museums, art galleries, hotels, castles and now, I can say, on top of a mountain. Guestbooks can also be a reminder of finitude. After all, once you scribble your name into a guestbook, unless you come back to the same place with great regularity, you'll never see your entry ever again. My name will be one more among all the people to have signed them. Unless they are digitized, and some future relative of mine scours online archives in search of references to me, the chances that anyone connected to me – living or yet to live – will encounter the marks I've made in these guestbooks are slim enough. This set me to thinking as to their purpose. Guestbooks work as a kind of intermittent census of yourself. A record of your movements for others. The word guestbook was first used in 1849 in *Graham's*, a magazine that was at one time a rival to *Harper's* and was edited by Edgar Allan Poe. The term 'visitor's book' appeared three years before in *Punch*. 'He plunged into the mysteries of the guestbook', ran a sentence in the February 1849 edition of *Graham's*. And we've been plunging in ever since. Outside of museums and exhibits, I associate a guestbook mostly with hotels. Not just any hotel. Hotels that were once country piles – expensive, but not showy, with a certain regard for their own place in history, however minor or major. Such guestbooks have an off-white or creamy paper, gold leaf about the edges of the pages, with a soft red leather cover – real or faux. I haven't yet been the first to sign an empty guestbook. In a way, I'm glad of this. The guestbook after all is a physical, bound, lined manifestation of the love people have for an exhibit, a hotel, or their friends and their cabin. What could be more unloved than a hotel with an empty or near-empty guestbook? What says decline more than huge gaps between one entry and the next? Only very rarely have I signed a guestbook at the end of its life, when there is just a page or two remaining. I have signed most somewhere in their middle age. There is a fullness to them; there are plenty of pages filled already, and pages as yet unfilled, waiting for fresh marks and remarks. Presented with a guestbook, I catch myself glancing immediately at the names just above where I will mark my entry. A neighbourly relationship is forming. I am interested first in rifling back through three or four of the closest pages, to find places I recognize. Occasionally, I hope to glimpse someone who comes from the same place I do. Then I look at names – seeking out the rare, the unusual. I marvel at the handwriting: the chicken scrawls, the cutesy and the cartoonish, the perfect cursive of those taught to write in close proximity to the teacher's cane. Some people leave a lot of themselves behind on the page. Full addresses, the numbers of their houses, postcodes and all. Some are more cryptic: a street or a town name, sometimes the country alone. Full names, initials, degrees, titles. Some leave little messages – congratulations on the wonderful exhibit, what wonderful hosts, how helpful the hotel staff were. Some draw smiley faces. Some use the guestbook as a chance to play or to chide. Some add the time. Many of course leave nothing, their visit logged, if at all, only in their memory. Writing in a guestbook is at once all about saying: *I was here – I lived, visited this place once, saw this exhibit*, but it is also strangely anonymous as an act. No one is ever likely to read what you've written and yet you hope. After a few days, a few weeks, to say nothing of the passing of years, your entry will be beyond the onward march of the guestbook pages. The ubiquity of the guestbook serves as a reminder that we are all guests, wherever we go. Take pleasure in the plunge as often as you can.

Wa(l)king: morning, night

It's been a long winter. I have found myself short of breath. Short of a lot. Life has felt short. My walking has been curtailed. I tried to keep a diary of my walks and it was as abrupt as some of the walks. Here is another attempt.

I HAVE LEARNED a lot about my heart on walks. Learned how to approach hills, and when to take breaks. Nobody has taught me more on my walks than my dog, though. Not long after first moving to Norway, within less than a year, Miriam and I bought a dog. As a joke, but feeling a little homesick, I suggested we call her 'Madra', the Irish for dog. In truth, the move to Norway had been hard. Those first six months were the toughest: my small savings disappeared quickly, my job was poorly paid. It was stressful to arrive in a country in which I didn't speak the language for the second time in two years. As my cardiologist in Norway once pointed out, most people with my condition don't tend to move from their place of birth. Madra the dog. Two-syllable words are great for calling a dog back. Madra was perfect. She is grey and white with wolf-like markings. A Jämthund. A Swedish breed of *elghund*. A dog for hunting moose. Madra is bred to hunt: she is a working dog and needs plenty of exercise all year round. It means that I don't have to motivate myself to get up and go out. The dog needs walking and we don't need shit in our living room. It brings me into the woods on the north-west of Oslo daily. Having a dog is the best thing imaginable for someone with a congenital heart defect. A wonderful companion for what can be a lonely disease, and it can be a low-impact way of getting the exercise you need. I am happy, the dog is happy.

DOG WALKING IS NOTHING like walking by yourself. Daily, ritualized, regular as meals. It requires a different kind of attention. It takes longer before you can both hit your stride and each forget the other. There is more stopping to smell, if not the flowers, then whatever secret signals other dogs have left behind. This is the great pleasure of snow for dog owners. Snow reveals to us what the spring and summer conceal. It makes visible the animal traces that crisscross walking paths, the footprints of hares, the piss of other dogs. Snow as revelator. Olfactory unmasker.

THE DANGER OF DOG walks is that they become perfunctory. They take place twice a day, at least. A standing engagement. They can quickly lose their lustre. It is Tuesday morning and -15 degrees outside. There is fresh snow on the ground. 7 a.m. It won't be light for another two hours. You have to walk the dog and get home in time to shower, eat breakfast and leave for work. Some days these walks take on the unpleasant feeling of a chore. You have to find some small pleasure in them. Rarely do you hit a rhythm. The loop is short. The only other walkers out are other dog owners. There is no easy sociability at this hour, no stopping for bum-sniffs. Just nodded acknowledgement that sometimes we'd rather not be moving our legs and propelling ourselves forward into the day. Amid the routine, there might be the hint of a wild animal, a flash of fur near the tree line or a set of footsteps traced in the snow, that make it memorable.

I NEARLY STEP in dogshit. I can barely distinguish it from the mulch of autumn leaves. It doesn't belong to Madra, so it repulses me. I get anxious about the surveillance machine in my pocket, counting my steps. I think about the forest. About the view over the city. Madra sniffs the ground. Madra is only troubled that she is on a leash. Neither of us, even in the free fresh air, is entirely free.

I ALMOST NEVER WALK without my mobile phone these days, in my pocket or in my hand. I use its less-than-accurate step counter to obsessively check my progress. In my first job in Norway, at an Irish pub, I clocked close to 16,000 steps a day and could eat like a horse. Now I have a desk job again and need to move my body more, but it gets harder and harder. I am weak. I want to know how many steps I've taken. I want to feel the little hit that tells me I've passed my step count for the day. I am desperate to validate my own meagre exercise. I keep thinking that if I can just go on another couple of thousand steps, I can buy some more time in the future where my heart won't trouble me.

My phone died one Sunday and I couldn't find my charger. I decided to go to a café all the way across the city where a friend had started working. It was my first time going there and I had only the vaguest sense of where it was. I had to rely on the internal map of the city I had built up inside myself in the past couple of years, which was patchy. It was difficult to think of myself as not being at the centre of the map, the little blue dot moving about on a screen, but as a body moving through a city, not flat and abstract but concrete. Oslo is the first city I learned to navigate entirely by phone. Built out in a circumference from the water and bounded to the north and east by thick woods that stretch right back to Harestua where I first lived, Oslo is ringed by large motorways inside of which there are streets in grids. I have always lived in places cut by rivers before. Here there is also a thin river, street-wide at most, that cuts the city from east to west; but for me, Oslo is what happens between the water and the woods. I never quite have my bearings. I wanted to give up using my phone to get from A to B, to trust my feet to guide me again.

IN SO MANY WORDS, I deleted the stars. I have opened out the city again. I have decoupled myself from the map. Made it possible to get lost. The corners of the city soften at the edges. The hard and soft copy of the streets at odds. My feet are my repository, my archive of movement. Memories become pathways. I have nowhere to go tonight.

THE SLEET CUTS ACROSS my face and covers Madra's fur in crystal. The hillside swirls ahead. We turn back, hugging the road sheltered from the wind. I think about a cup of tea. I have no idea what Madra is thinking.

Overground station. We enclose ourselves. Corrode the common.

TH-DUNK TH-DUNK DUNK DUNK. *th-dunk th-dunk dunk dunk.* My heart hammers. As if it were going to burst through the skin of my chest. I clam up. Sweat. Uphill. Minor incline. Breakfast squeezes my breathing.

I CAN'T TELL the time in the winter. Night lasts most of the day. Cloud cover and fog conspire with rain to envelop the hillside on which we live looking down over Oslo. I keep walks with Madra short. The forest nearby is full of people sledding in the snow. Already as I walk in this awful weather, I think about getting up to walk Madra again tomorrow. And the day after.

I FEEL OLDER TODAY. I feel myself ageing. I can't muster the energy to go much farther down the hill from our apartment in Oslo to a metro station about twenty minutes away and then get the metro back with the dog. I am embarrassed by my lack of fitness, at the shallowness of my breathing. Madra looks bored.

TIRED. But honestly that could just be the darkness. Madra and I go outside but we don't like it. It isn't even that it's wet. It isn't even that it is cold. We just aren't bothered. It is a walk only insofar as our feet propel us forward briefly. It ends abruptly.

SEAN BONNEY IS DEAD. That wasn't true when I went out walking. I came home, saw the news and started reading. I reach for his books in his absence. The poems that bring me back to Cork, to London. I think I should go out into the city and carry some poems in my pockets. Maybe I should give them out to friends like flowers for the dead. *Our Death*. I won't be walking Madra this evening. She went searching for dead things in the neighbours' gardens for hours. I won't be able to show my face for days. I don't mind, but she might.

SOMETIMES, like last night, I sit up and read medical journal articles about congenital heart defects and their impact on people who grow up with them. It starts out small. I read until my eyes are heavy and I'm reading the same words over and over. Then I put my phone down on my bedside locker and turn over to go to sleep. I turn to one side then the other, trying to avoid the beat of my heart. Hearing it, I begin to cycle through scenarios about what might happen to me. I spiral. I roll over to get my phone. I search for reassuring stories about transposition of the great arteries in adults. I skim-read academic articles, half-understanding them. Sometimes it helps, sometimes it makes it worse. I put my phone down. Try to sleep. Pick my phone up. Google again. Skim. Set my phone down again. Eventually, exhausted though not relieved, I sleep.

I HAVE BEEN THINKING a lot about my diet lately. Not just food. Not just drink. TV shows, movies, music, books. I have been – again – thinking about dying.

A LOT OF WHAT I watch and read and listen to teaches me that illness is a personal failing. I, like many others who have been labelled disabled or chronically ill, am socialized to see it as a fight. I am supposed to see myself as a warrior. Brave. But if you've ever been seriously sick, you know that you are overcome with fear. When I am not brave, when I don't have any fight in me, I feel like I'm letting the side down. But that is bullshit. I am tired of putting a brave face on it. I am going for a walk.

ONE OF THE BEST days in my life was the day I no longer received disability allowance. I started on it during the heady days of the Celtic Tiger. Standing in a queue at the post office with everyone else on the day the payment came out made me feel like a social outcast. Shame is a weapon wielded in many aspects of life. I felt it then. I burned with horrible embarrassment over receiving these payments. The same shame I was made to feel when initially seeking this social safety net that was mine and many others' right. Eventually it was possible for the payment to be made directly to your bank account. Eventually instead of ashamed I got angry. A person's worth is not judged their ability to work. I got through college thanks to my disability allowance and afterwards found a job, part-time lecturing and later working an admin role at the college. It was the first of many half-jobs I would work for the next few years: teaching English as a foreign language (both on and off the books), proofreading for a terrible e-learning company. Each job I've had has put greater distance between me and the humiliation I felt when applying for disability allowance. When I got to Norway with no Norwegian, no one wanted to know me, workwise. After almost two months without work, and with only my daily walks through the woods at Harestua to keep me sane, I got a job in an Irish bar. This was a whole new kind of movement. It was walking but not like I had ever done before: with plates in hand, or clearing glasses, moving between the four bars on crazy packed days, pouring pint after pint. It was thrilling and exhausting. I had never been on my feet so much but I was so glad I felt able to do it. Sometimes though I was so worn out by the end of my shift that my legs hurt like hell. Then I would come home and be so tired that I was cranky to Miriam and quick to walk Madra. Walking lost its pleasurable, leisurely quality. My feet were burning already. I knew I couldn't do it for ever. And having a heart defect in an environment soaked with alcohol could never last. I would never last. Eventually, I found a job in an office. Every job and every piece of work I've done has been my insistence that being *dis*abled is a narrow category. I am plenty able. I am able for life and what it throws at me.

I WALK ALONG the pier in Oslo during my lunch break with my headphones on. I think about the fighter's attitude that is expected of me, as though it's merely a matter of outlook that will change something fundamental to my person. Being tough, being a warrior: I hate all this language that people are encouraged to use when discussing illness. You can be sick, but you cannot admit to being weak. The tension between toughness and reality reveals itself in the face of congenital illness. I can no more 'defeat' transposition of the great arteries than change my eye colour or my height.

I SIGN UP FOR a one-day course for men born with heart conditions at the hospital I attend for my yearly checkups. A chance for men like me to talk to social workers and to each other about the problems we face. A doctor will talk mainly about the physiological. But long-term illnesses carried from birth leave scars on thought as well as skin. They are constant companions. I have to live with them every day – the effects of illness.

THE ONE-DAY COURSE isn't until April which seems like for ever away. I am hoping to find a new lease of life. I have spent too much of my life ignoring my condition. The condition is like a friend I've known so long that I didn't feel the need to keep up with it. But that isn't as true as it used to be; I need to become acquainted with it again. I need to meet other people who have this same friend in order to know it better. I am dreading being open in front of a group. I am terrified of what to say. I practise my speech in both Norwegian and English in my head over and over, for when it's my turn to speak, trying to get across the feelings that come with this. I can already see myself choking up, crying. I will have to ugly-cry. Either before, during or after.

I HAVE STOPPED DRINKING coffee, almost. I want, as always, to give up alcohol. I don't drink very much but I need to learn how to socialize in bars without it. It is much easier here in Norway than in Ireland. Many social activities here are alcohol-free. I obsess about what I eat and drink. I worry about the cumulative effects of everything. Every bar of chocolate that should have been fruit. Every fizzy drink that should have been water. And not just because it's Sunday and I was out until 3 a.m. last night with friends. This is probably not the state in which to write this stuff. Or perhaps it is ideal. I am tender and vulnerable. I am open.

AHEAD OF THE MEETING in April, I have a checkup on the third of February. I will be on my own. Miriam can't make it as she is starting her new job. For the first time in Norway, I will meet my specialist alone at the hospital. I will have to use English, I think, for some of it. I have questions. I have fears that need to be assuaged. And then I will go to work after. I'll answer phone calls and emails and wait for the day to end. I'll go home to Madra and relax. I'll take her for a walk. Down as far as Vinderen maybe. Or maybe I'll try to go uphill. The evenings at least are lengthening.

IN THE SMALL HOURS, I have been reading medical journal articles again. I don't know what I'm looking for – that somewhere between the literature review and methodology I will find a guerrilla insertion from one of the authors to say that things will be okay? A message written to all of us, sitting up late at night, anxious, typing search terms into Google. According to one article I pull up, reading in the hopes that it will calm me down, the authors note that the psychological impact of living with a congenital heart defect is among the most stressful parts of this condition.

ACCORDING TO ANOTHER – or maybe it's the same one, I don't really remember, I read these when I cannot sleep – having sex is about as strenuous as going up two flights of stairs. So I shouldn't worry so much, apparently. I wish I had known this when I was seventeen.

I TRY TO IMAGINE the path of my mind if it didn't always circle back to my heart condition. What it would look like. What would populate the edges of the path. Not old X-ray images, not MRI scans, not scar tissue, not ECG printouts, not prescriptions. I wonder if I can get a handle on this illness so that the panic it induces in me every few months is no longer there. If I can move beyond the need to google late at night for some sign that things might not always be so hard. I wonder, can I ever come to know myself? Whenever I feel I've gotten a handle on this thing, something shifts. This duplicitous partner of mine. A constant uphill battle in other words. It is exhausting. I am exhausted. I am ready for winter to end and spring to arrive. I am ready for sunlight. I am ready for a gear change. I am waiting to get married.

I STRUGGLE WITH NOT wanting to sound like I fall back on my condition. Still, to deny my heart would be to deny my reality. I have learned the difference between what society thinks illness is or ought to be and my own experience of it. Nonetheless, some of these modes of thinking are deeply ingrained from the years of passive reception of ideas that a person's sickness is their own fault. The weight of personal responsibility in the neoliberal age is everywhere, especially places where it doesn't belong. I struggle to find self-acceptance in the face of a desire to not come across as weak. I have always tried not to let my illness be the dominating factor in my life. To make it clear that I have an illness, but that I am not my illness. This vitally important distinction. I cling to it. Even though at every turn it has been. It has shaped me completely. Whatever authority I have tried to exert over it has been futile. It informs every decision to the point where I cannot decouple from it.

FEBRUARY. At the meeting the cardiologist expresses concern. It seems I have developed an arrythmia – an irregular heart-beat. Not unusual in transposition patients but it will mean intervention beyond just medicine. They will have to try electro-cardioversion therapy. Failing that, that failing: ablation. Then perhaps a pacemaker. I am mute. I am terrified. I feel old suddenly. I don't remember the walk home from the hospital afterwards.

I AM TIRED, breathless. Suddenly sleepy at a moment's notice. I can't eat. I am on the verge of throwing up regularly. Miriam has moved out of Oslo for her new job. She has been looking for work for so long. A year almost. We are so happy when she gets the job in Dokka. Things have been tight for so long. It is nearly three hours away by bus. Neither of us drive. We've never had to before. She starts renting in Dokka, I keep our flat in Oslo. We make plans for weekends together: every other weekend, here or there. We call in the evenings during the week. We scatter some of her grandmother's ashes in February. I cough and cough. My mother and father start cocooning. The world closes. Airports and city squares empty. I don't get my ablation in March. I don't get the chance to express myself in April. Too much happens.

# Calendar

**21 March 2020**

*Miriam, 18:02*

Hey – David's just visited A&E and they're going to admit him to hospital. I'm on my way to Oslo now and I'll let you know of any updates. Is there anything I can do for you?

*Maria, 18:18*

Not really Miriam in normal circumstances I would fly over. Let me know as soon as you see him. I was going to ring him today but you know he don't like fussing.

**23 March 2020**

*Maria, 21:04*

Hi Miriam I got Linda to ring the hospital I was feeling a bit wobbly and not up to it. The same as you said he's squeezing their hands when they ask and his temperature has come down from 40.7 to 40.4. The nurse was saying doctor is in around 11 in morning and better ringing after that. He is doing everything they are asking, so I'm feeling a bit more positive. Xx

*Miriam, 21:46*
Glad to hear his temperature is coming down.
Take care of yourself.

## 24 March 2020

*Miriam, 11:30*

Hi Maria – just talked to the nurse and a doctor. Very similar to last night, they're working most on getting his fever down, and trying him on a different set of antibiotics.

*Maria, 13:41*

[Forwarded] Spoke to the nurse his temp went up over 41 degrees they're using a cooling machine to bring this down and it's now at 39.9 so under control. They have him sedated as it be too uncomfortable to use this if you are awake. His oxygen levels are good at 45% both yesterday and today. They will do another chest x-ray to keep an eye on this. His heartbeat is all good too. They have him on antibiotics in case of bacterial infection.

*Miriam, 13:42*

Oh so good to hear its under 40 now

*Maria, 19:28*

[Forwarded] Hi everyone just called the hospital great news his temp is down to 38 blood pressure is stable and they are still happy with his oxygen levels. They will probably keep him on the cooling machine again tomorrow just to be sure. Had his chest xray but the results weren't back yet, I'll check on this again in the morning. Overall they are happy but as she said things go up and down in ICU but good positives there for today.

Linda just sent this good positive there. Hope your okay Miriam, have you symptoms

*Miriam, 19:43*
I was a bit sick yesterday but I've taken some paracetamol
and fell much better today in general

*Miriam, 11:51*
Temperature down to 37.6 otherwise nothing new :)

*Maria, 11:53*
Fantastic news Miriam. Hope your still ok.

*Maria, 12:00*
*[Forwarded]* Well spoke with nurse and I think this might be start of new shift of nurses. She said he was stable overnight. He's waking a little and he's trying to take out the breathing tube so they have to sedate him. He has a chest xray every-day to keep an eye on things. Temp is still down at 38. I'll call again this evening. Stable is good tho.

Linda just sent this Miriam

*Miriam, 12:02*
Thumbs up.

*Miriam, 18:51*
Just called the hospital again, and they said there's very little change in how he's doing. They'll know more about the antibiotics tomorrow, but in the meantime it sounds like he's very stable

## 26 March 2020

*Maria, 19:39*
[*Forwarded*] David's temp went up again so they put him back on cooling machine and it's gone back down to 38. He is responsive to the nurse nodding and squeezing her hand. They're hoping to take him off breathing tube tomorrow but will depend on how he does tonite. They are happy overall still. Not sure if they told you abot temperature

*Miriam, 19:40*
They had said it went up a tiny bit again but not that they had put him back on the cooling machine

*Maria, 19:42*
Let's hope it stays down

*Miriam, 19:42*
Yeah well with the infection improving I'd hope it will

*Maria, 19:44*
More prayers

*Miriam, 19:47*
Did I tell you my dad's wife's sister has her whole southern baptist church praying for david

*Maria, 19:49*
He'll have to start going to mass again.

*Miriam, 19:49*
Haha!!

*Maria, 20:02*
I can imagine what he would say.

**27 March 2020**

*Maria, 19:12*
[*Forwarded*] Good news again from the hospital. His blood results are showing lower levels of the infection. His breathing is good with some help from the ventilator. They're saying that he can hear them so I asked nurse to tell him we all said hello and to keep getting stronger. Temp still at 38 but still off the cooling machine. They are hoping he'll be even more awake tomorrow.

*Miriam, 19:13*
So good to hear

**29 MARCH 2020**

*Maria, 12:30*
Just spoke to hospital he's sitting up and getting physiotherapy. He is communicating by writing so that is great. He's still on ventilator. Temp is still at 39 but they are working on that. Great to hear he's writing.

**30 March 2020**

*Maria, 12:15*
He is trying to pull out the tube, they could do it another way but can't because of the virus

*Miriam, 12:16*
I'm not surprised he's trying to remove it he's not very good with pain. Hopefully they can take it out in a day or two

*Maria, 12:21*
No he wouldn't be a great patient. Linda told nurse to tell him do as he's told lol. It should be out by end of week. Hope your keeping well x

*Miriam, 13:07*
It's up and down with me. I think the waiting was getting to me so I called a friend last night and had a good cry. Feels very helpless sometimes, but I feel better now.

*Maria, 13:25*
Yes it is the not knowing how long it is going to go on for. It must be very hard for you on your own at least I have Johnny to drive me mad and contradicting one another, it keeps me going.

I GOT COVID-19. We're not sure where. It was the earliest days of it in Norway then. I remember nothing real from that time. Sometimes, I look back at the messages I was sending friends and my partner the day or two before I finally went to the A&E in Oslo. It's as if someone else wrote them. The A&E is its own building in the city centre. If they cannot treat you there, they send you to one of the city's hospitals. Once the nurses realized I had the coronavirus, I was taken by ambulance to the hospital nearest to where I lived in the city. I remember almost nothing about the ambulance rides. I was in and out of consciousness, ferried first to one hospital and then to another. First from the A&E in the city centre to Diakonhjemmet Hospital and then to Rikshospitalet. One thing I knew was that I had to tell them at Diakonhjemmet that I had a congenital heart defect. That I needed more care than most. I have no idea how I got the words out. I remember the red brick, an archway at Diakonhjemmet. The luminous colour of the ambulance. The strength of the light inside it. When I came to, I was in a fever, burning, stripped of my clothes. I thought I was in a war zone, surrounded by doctors from Norway and Japan. I was constantly thirsty. My teeth felt as though they had collapsed in on themselves. I couldn't eat anything. I believed my hair had all fallen out. In my vision my fingers were deformed and discoloured. I writhed in pain as I tried to sleep and they put cooling patches all over my body to reduce my temperature. I believed there was a secret room nearby where people were being euthanized. The clocks on the walls had twelve at every position. Above us they dangled metal question marks from the ceiling, seemingly to mock us and ask *when will you die?* Among the hallucinations I imagined a Nazi doctor was a member of the team caring for me. I remember looking at a screen full of blinking lights that I decided indicated which patients were staying and those who had been selected to be deprogrammed. I believed that I had been chosen. I would come before a panel. Eight doctors and me. They would assess my fitness to be saved. We would walk in the grounds of the hospital and talk, arguing like Romans. We would not be dressed so that we could all be honest with one another. There could be no hiding behind our clothed identities. I spent the time in the ICU awaiting my date to be seen by the panel of eight doctors. I had guessed that given my heart condition, I would not be considered worth saving. Drinks morphed in my hands from water to coffee to lemonade. All I wanted was ice. The roof of my mouth was always dry. I asked continually for pen and paper to write my final testament. They could not give them to me as it might be contaminated with the disease and they would have to destroy anything I touched immediately after it left my isolated room. I was not allowed any open windows. Every moment, every movement, took great effort. I thought I felt my lungs collapse. The light going out.

At one point, as I imagined it, my bed was moved into a room full of doctors working silently on computers. Then gunfire. I leaped from my bed to evade the bullets that were flying in through the windows of this hospital, which I thought was no hospital at all but a facility for the remaking of death. I came down from the ICU in a haze with days missing, still not believing I was really in Oslo. Everything seemed shiny and new. When I spoke to Miriam on the phone, I told her about my terror and wondered how my body would survive the journey back to Norway. I said goodbye forever more than once on the phone to my mother. When I hung up, I'd look outside at people jogging, cycling, at red city buses going by on their regular routes. I thought the buildings outside were a simulacrum, a convincing fake to allay the fears of the inmates. I asked a nurse why she'd volunteered to come so far when she talked about her children. I asked her, did she not miss them? She told me she saw them every night. I could not quite believe it. I thought they had replicated the city beyond the hospital and that we were on an island in a distant country. It took them two days to convince me otherwise.

First, the new room I move into after the ICU – a journey that seems to take for ever to me, passing under lit corridors and glass roofs – feels large and airy but I still see bullet holes forming on the walls. It is hard to move much. My fingers are still discoloured. I keep touching my head to check my hair is there. I drink a diluted berry drink with lots of ice in it. I try to eat a yoghurt. I cannot control my bowels. I am fed a protein-heavy mix via drip to get my strength up. The nurses come in regularly with bedpans and wash my body as best they can. I spend a lot of time on my stomach. A poster on the wall outlining Covid procedures among the nurses (destroying their PPE after being in the room, hand-washing) is, I imagine, a poster for a farewell concert in my memory. The nurse looks at me like I'm crazy. Only after staring at it for a long time do the real words on this little poster come into view. I may be in Oslo now, but my mind still thinks I'm dying. I ask the doctors and nurses incessantly if I'm going to die. I talk to some of them about their families, their hours on shifts. As best I can make out, I am the only person on the cardiology ward with Covid-19. My phone isn't working. I can't get it to charge. I don't know where my watch is. I cannot get up. I have a catheter in my wrist. One of my nurses is exhausted on his shift, though they seem to need everyone, even this guy who has a new-born child at home. He doesn't get much sleep and neither do I. I watch documentaries on NRK2. A two-part show about Grieg's lyric pieces, another about A. O. Vinje, a journalist who was the first to write more in Norwegian dialect than Danish. I ask over and over again if I'm going to die.

**31 March 2020**

*Miriam, 17:43*

They've just finished moving him to cardiology. They've said to call in a few hours so I'll do that tonight. I also mentioned he's a bit depressed and they said that's very normal in this type of situation but as he gets better he'll start feeling more himself

*Maria, 17:51*

Glad it's cardiology. Okay Miriam we won't ring tonight I'll leave it until tomorrow. Let me know how you get on

*Maria, 20:52*

He just rang me. He's not in a good place. He said he only has 50/50 chance of surviving. He is in a very dark place at the moment. He got tired very quickly. I tried to encourage him to keep fighting.

*Miriam, 20:53*

Okay. Hopefully he's just being grumpy about being ill.

**2 April 2020**

*Miriam, 11:08*

It sounds like his fever is nice and low today – but they're monitoring his heart rate and blood oxygen levels to get them back to his previous levels

*Maria, 17:38*

Miriam spoke to David he is sounding like himself tg. He got tired but that was after 15mins. He is doing exercise but legs not good, it will take time. I told him we will be over as soon as possible and safe. He had tea and toast for breakfast but he couldn't eat after that. Baby steps every day.

**3 April 2020**

Just off the phone with david – if he keeps getting better at this rate the doctors said he might be out in 10 days or so

## 4 APRIL 2020

*Maria, 10:33*

Great Miriam. He was saying he was bored yesterday, good sign. Did he get to try standing today. If I ask too many questions about his legs he will get annoyed with me

*Maria, 11:33*

I set the begonia last Saturday when David wasn't good, instead of prayers I thought when they are flowering David and yourself will be sitting out in your garden.

**6 April 2020**

*Miriam, 11:31*
They're not sure if there will be any long term damage to his lungs but I think David is looking forward to slowing his life down a little anyways.

**7 April 2020**

*Miriam, 12:29*
David's coming home today –
we're on our way to hospital now

*Maria, 12:48*
I'm so so happy tears of joy

THERE IS A CALENDAR inside my head. It won't be long now until the races & summer's end. Spring begins on Brigid's Day, even here where the snow says different. My body feels the shifting seasons, frequency out of step with the place through which it moves. Scrambled. Family birthdays anchor me.

Each empty white box an endless possibility, each flattened with time. Each has the chance to become permanently fixed. That was the day that. I'll always remember it, it was the Saturday before I was due to. Packed and unpacked.

We add to these boxes. Your birthday. Our first date. The date we bought our first house. The day we wed. But I have trouble fixing other days: *Rosh Hashanah, Kristi Himmelfartsdag*. The King's birthday. May Day is more reliable.

Memory bank & motion. Roll call of living & of dead. Inside these white boxes.

### 21 March 2020
Britain and Ireland adopted the Gregorian calendar in September 1752. The calendar was first introduced in 1582 by Pope Gregory XIII and adopted intermittently across Europe. Hugh O'Neill, Earl of Tyrone, an early adopter, dated his letters in the 'New Style'. For instance, one endorsed copy of his letters was dated 7 December 1597 but received from him in November 1597. The use of a new calendar, a defiant move. It would die out with the Earl and his rebellion.

This New Style calendar was adopted in Norway and Denmark in the year 1700. Those who went to bed before midnight of 18 February awoke to a new day, a new date: 1 March 1700. I was born on 19 February, so dates in or near it always hold an additional interest to me. I cast myself back to imagine what it would be like to have been born on 19 February in a given year.

The tropic of Pisces begins on 19 February, ending on 20 March. As I was born on 19 February and nearly died on 21 March, the day after the tropic – my tropic shifted. I ordered a taxi to the emergency room. I was placed in an ambulance. I called you. That night, becoming delirious, I was intubated, induced into a coma. I called you on the phone. I had to cut the call short to go in, to go under. I woke up eleven days later, eleven kilos lighter. Like the angry people of Britain in 1752, I lost eleven days, and I too am scrambling to get them back. I, too, am angry at my loss.

**7 April 2020**
I was supposed to be in Berlin that evening, to give a reading at the Curious Fox. Instead, I stumbled down a back stairwell out of Rikshospitalet and into your arms, nurses in their PPE guiding me by one arm. Guiding me into your arms and the few feet along the path into your mother's car. Through the crossing at Slemdal and home into bed with a book on Italian cinema.

There was a calendar in the bedroom from the Office of Public Works. I got it at the start of the year and began crossing off the days, putting in dates for upcoming gigs, our travel plans, my readings. Over the dates 21 March–7 April any writing of mine, my scrawl, is replaced by the neat, steady marker of your hand, detailing my hospitalization. On certain days you write 'fever down from 41 to 38' or 'focus on blood/oxygen'. On others 'bored', with a smiley face. Here I see my eleven missing days, filled in, an arrow drawn by you breaking the walls of the little white boxes. A continuity at odds with my own hexed memory of those days. The parallel days we lived then: not in Edinburgh as planned, nor Glasgow, but me in bed, gaining my strength again, regaining.

Intervention

THOSE FIRST STEPS from the side of my bed, in those mixed-up March and April days, were the longest walks I've ever taken. At first even standing up was exhausting. I learned to stand again with a nurse to either side of me. One of them collected Elvis records and was a long-distance cyclist. To stand up and stay standing was an effort that took all my might. To place one foot in front of the other, the most basic mechanism, were first laborious shuffles. Just to get to the bathroom, no more than ten paces from the bed, legs like lead, seemed impossibly far. When I saw myself in the mirror, I was a ghost, my cheeks hollowed out. My arms, shoulders, legs, thin as branches. Where was the person who had walked parts of the old King's Road? The miles and miles to the feet of Gaustatoppen? The Waterford Greenway all the way to Dungarvan?

*PATIENT*: this word rooted in suffering. The suffering comes not from what keeps me in hospital but from the diminished life of the ward. My impatience. After the horror of Covid-19, I am coming back to the hospital again. My heart has an arrhythmia. They try to correct with a simple procedure: an ablation. It works, but only briefly. My heart's rhythm is described by the doctor as anarchic. I will have to get a pacemaker. I will be brought into the hospital again; it is a short downhill walk from the apartment we are renting. They will open a little pouch in my skin and thread leads around my heart. I feel like I have moved into the hospital. In the corridors, nurses recognize me, but behind their facemasks, shorn of the PPE in which they first cared for me, I cannot recall them by their eyes alone.

Under pandemic restrictions, we cannot have visitors on the cardiology ward, just like when I was recovering from the coronavirus in April. It's summertime now and the sun shines long and late into the night. It hardly gets dark, even here in Oslo. It looks glorious outside. Warm, cloying almost, but windless – perfect for a walk. I'd love to go from my room here towards Sognsvann, a lake not far off. I am an emotional wreck and cannot imagine I will ever get out of hospital again. I frighten the medical staff with my despair. They sense the fear in me. My eyes feel as though they are wild and unfocused. The doctor says he's not sure how long they'll have to keep me in. This makes me frantic. They give me my own room so I don't have to put a brave face on it. Though I couldn't if I wanted to. The hospital chaplain comes to see me one morning. We talk, I tell her about the house we plan to buy, the village we are moving to. The future I cannot imagine. We talk, in English and Norwegian, each of us grasping across the allocated distance of the small room.

IT TAKES TIME to settle into the role of patient. To tug the cord by the bedside when things are not as they might be. When I throw up and get dizzy and don't want to admit it. Enforced leisure is a form of torture. I read books half-heartedly. I read lots of poetry, short stories, magazines, newspapers. Books I know like old friends. Or at least, like friends I haven't seen since I was seventeen. *East of Eden.*

I WALK THE CORRIDORS of the ward, somnambulant. I am weighed down by the telemetry machine hanging heavy from my neck which connects to nodes puckering my chest, measuring my heart rate. I trace the T-shape of the corridors, turning right past the nurses' station down to the small balcony where sometimes patients, sometimes paramedics smoke. Turning at the glass doors, I go in a straight line, again past the nurses' station and continue straight, looking at framed photos that adorn the walls between doors leading to supply and medicine closets, offices, isolated bedrooms for patients. At the end of this corridor, I turn back and make for the nurses' station again, turning right past the little canteen where we get our food and drink, and again into my room. I do this two, three times a day. This little walk. One of the nurses who looks in on me a lot tells me to slow down, that I don't need to be speeding along, trying so hard. But I want to walk right out of there. The only thing that's stopping me is the weight around my neck, this damned telemetry machine.

MIRIAM IS NOT ALLOWED to come and see me. I am back in hospital and it is midweek. Those first two weeks I got home after Covid, I could hardly walk, or do anything for myself. I can remember how weak I was cutting a loaf of bread. Cracking and frying an egg was a milestone. I kneaded some dough to make bread and needed to lie down afterwards. When at home again, at first I could only drink water and ginger ale. I drank ginger ale by the litre. My stomach had shrunk and so had my appetite. I was so desperate to eat something other than hospital food, so grateful to be home that I asked Miriam to make me a stew. I couldn't eat it. It was too rich. For days all I could eat was bland, beige food. It tasted amazing to my destroyed taste buds, my tongue that was sore, repairing itself slowly. My viciously chapped lips. For the longest time I had no sense of smell. Eating was physically uncomfortable. I had sores on my body from laying in the hospital bed for so long. I needed a chair in the shower. I cried at nothing and could not go outside for weeks. I was unable to walk from one end of our small apartment to the other. Miriam took time out from her new job to mind me for almost a month and work part-time from home. I was triggered by everything, even episodes of *Community*. Eventually, she had to go back to her job in Dokka. I was left to look after myself, waiting to go back to hospital.

On my return visit to the hospital in June I am allowed visitors. I inform the nurses of who is due to come see me so the list of visitors can be brought down to security. Miriam can't come so her mother visits instead, bringing McDonald's, contraband in my eyes, which to my amazement the nurses don't object to. We video call Miriam and the three of us eat dinner together in this augmented reality, us stinking out the hospital room with quarter pounders with cheese, and Miriam in her short-term apartment. My friend Paddy comes by another day. We sit out in the common area and chat about football. These visits give shape to the endless days. Up, wash, breakfast back in my room, a boiled egg usually, a mini bread roll, some liver pâté or cream cheese on *knekkebrød*. Tea. Orange juice. Then the long morning, reading. Lunch early, like Norwegians do, around 11.30 or midday, dinner at 4.30 p.m., then people can stop by from about 5.30 p.m. I have learned how to be a patient now. I have learned to pass the idle hours with reams of TV. There is free Wi-Fi. I watch *Billions* on HBO.

THE FIRST TIME it was suggested that I might need a pacemaker was when I started my postgraduate studies at UCC. Then, I was most worried about having to take time out from college. How it would affect my studies. Now, a decade later, I feel my shoulders relax when I realize this will mean only a few more weeks of bed rest and not, as I had thought then, that it would bring my life to a halt indefinitely. But before having to return to the ward, we go on holidays. Miriam and I take Madra and go to Lillehammer. We find a dog-friendly room in a hotel there. We go to the art museum and to bookshops, and things almost seem normal for a few days. From there we go to the *hytte* and take long walks across the open land, traversing bogs and eyeing up the cloudberries, but we're a few weeks too early for picking. Only a handful are ripe. In my pocket is Gerry Loose's *The Great Book of the Woods*. A voice path.

I ARRIVE A THIRD time to the hospital. This time it is easier. I know the drill now. I know when dinner is served. What code to press on the microwave to heat the meals. Where the biscuits are hidden. The nurses know me and I get to know them. I have the rhythm of the place down. I come with my laptop loaded, podcasts saved, some magazines and poetry books. Billions has stopped mid-season because of the pandemic. I have nothing else to watch. This time, thankfully, I'm not hooked up to a telemetry unit, whose signal ranges only as far as the corridors. Instead, I am free to roam. This means that rather than being stuck to the ward for short looping walks, I am able to walk through the hospital grounds. I take *The Great Book of the Woods* with me.

THE HOSPITAL IS SITUATED next to Frogner river and the surrounding woodland. The trails and paths in the woods form part of the wider network of trails for walking and skiing that are maintained by the Norwegian Trekking Association and the Norwegian Skiing Association. They also have some of their own interventions on these trails. They provide places to stop and rest, sit and contemplate, do some outdoor exercise.

I AM WIDE AWAKE when they put a pacemaker inside my chest. They slice open a little pocket – I imagine it as a tiny pitta bread – and insert the wires and the little box with its battery. I lie straight on my back, dressed from the waist down, and a kind of tarp placed between my face and my chest so I can't see exactly what is going on below my neck. To my left, if I tilt my head enough, I can watch on the screen as the leads from the pacemaker are guided gently inside my body. I talk to one of the surgeons about golfing in Ireland, which he likes to do regularly, as he delicately places the wires for the pacemaker around my heart. We speak of how we have missed travel. Inside me they place a pacemaker. Altered rhythm. O my robot heart, bulging from my breast. Strange metronome of tempered song.

The Fresh Air Hospital

Since 2019, Rikshospitalet in Oslo has its own cabin. The cabin, or *hytte* in Norwegian, is an almost sacred space to people in Norway. Not everyone owns a cabin, but many people have access to one, either privately or through the Norwegian Trekking Association. The *hytte* is where many Norwegians spend most of their holidays – Easter, midterms, chunks of July. I moved to Norway in 2016, when everyone in the Anglosphere seemed to be obsessed with the idea of *hygge*. *Hygge*, the supposedly untranslatable sense of comfort and coziness associated especially with the Danes, but also a concept in wider Scandinavia, was briefly all over the press, along with tips on how to put more *hygge* into your life. My favourite article about this skewered the idea, saying that what you really wanted wasn't *hygge* but social democracy. But forget *hygge*, *hytte* is where it's really at. A hytte is the physical structure that embodies the feeling represented by *hygge*. It gives form to the formless. A *hytte* is a mountain or seaside cabin, usually reasonably rough and ready – although these days, newly built *hytte* often resemble second homes, tricked out with Wi-Fi etc. – to which you go on holidays and, in theory at least, escape the drudge of daily life and its pressures. When I go to the *hytte* this is precisely the experience I have. The one which I frequent most, belonging to Miriam's family, is up above the village of Tuddal in Telemark, and looks out to the mountains around Gaustatoppen. There is no

TV, there is no Wi-Fi, there is electricity but no running water, only a well and whatever water we bring with us. There is an outhouse for doing your business. A shed with tools and firewood. There are the books that are kept there and the books we bring up. A library of relaxed reading. Otherwise, there are beds and chairs and tables, a fridge and a cooker.

TIME DEVELOPS AN ELASTIC quality at the *hytte*. It is measured out not by the clock but by book chapters, when someone last threw a log on the fire, by the length of a walk. It is a place imbued with relaxation, although there is also work and maintenance to be carried out. I have shovelled feet of snow from its roof. Keeping it clean and ready for the next visit, stocked with firewood and toilet roll and bark for the outhouse, are all a part of the ritual of the *hytte*.

IT IS A SPACE for contemplation. A centre from which you can roam and return to. Home from home.

It is for this reason that Rikshospitalet commissioned the well-known architecture firm Snøhetta to build a patient-friendly *hytte* on the grounds of the hospital. It opened in 2019 and operates on a booking system. It is part of a wider concept of the *friluftssykehus* – the fresh air hospital, which includes the trails I walked in the hospital grounds while waiting to get my pacemaker fitted. The idea stems from the fact that to be in hospital, to be a patient, is to be dehumanized and medicalized. The hospital is an institution and institutions retain that policing quality, that dehumanizing of those subject to them, about which people before Foucault and since have written. But this *hytte* is a recognition that for people who are likely to have long stints in hospital, the prospect of a space that functions like a *hytte* will help them rediscover themselves as they are, not merely as patients, or as sick people. As whole people.

WHETHER IT IS to be found overlooking a mountain range, along a seashore, or by a small flowing river in the grounds of a hospital, crossing that threshold is an act of recovery: of the self, mental and physical.

Hearing begins with the heart. My heart spoke staccato, notes clustering in fitful fists. The art of recognizing its patterns will have to be relearned. O my robot heart: you play on the beat now, syncope forsaken for certainty. O robot heart, my love, will you alter my gait as I go?

Forward

ONE TIME at the cabin I heard the story of a man who built a house on a steep cliff in the Geirangerfjord, which snakes in from the west coast of Norway, north of Bergen. This man was old when he told the story to a younger version of the person who told it to me. Although the house was made from wood, he wanted a brick chimney. He got the bricks from a nearby village but with the road to the house so steep, he had to carry the bricks himself. And so, for days on end, he would walk down to the village, gather as many bricks as he could manage, sometimes up to 50 kilos at a time, and make his way back up this steep and winding cliff walk. When asked about this seemingly impossible feat – *How did you do it?* – he replied: *It is important to start on the right foot.*

As my feet drift in one direction, my mind drifts in another. Drifting feet and mind have their anchor, arm's length and shoulder height ahead. I lead with my left foot forward.

# Walking Companions

This book has been written over many years on many walks in various countries and would not have been possible without the support and encouragement of a great many people. First, my parents, Maria – for keeping all the letters and correspondence related to my hospital visits as a child – and my late father, Johnny; my siblings Sharon, Belinda, John, Colette and Georgina, and my extended family. Anna. Arne and Linda. Friends in Oslo who have kept Miriam and I sane: Áine, Derek, Paddy, Ina, Linn, Chris – *tusen takk*. To Anneliese Moffitt for so many conversations about living with illness. I am overwhelmed by the goodness of so many more, including my colleagues at the Embassy of Ireland where I work.

My thanks to Eimear, Laura and Claire at Banshee Press for their belief in the book and for guiding me expertly through the process of turning this into what you have before you. To the Arts Council of Ireland for their generous support of my writing.

A word of thanks also to my most regular walking companion: our lovely Swedish *elghund* Madra, who changed the way I walk and gets me out every day. To Turlough O'Riordan of the Royal Irish Academy for his help on the history of cardiac surgery in Ireland. To friends who have read this book including James Cummins, Daryl Leeworthy, and especially Ellen Dillon and Tim Mac Gabhann, who encouraged and expanded my own sense of what I was doing in writing this: thank you all.

My thanks to the staff, past and present, of Our Lady's Hospital for Sick Children at Crumlin and the Mater Hospital in Dublin – two places I was a patient for most of my life. To the wonderful staff of the GUCH unit, the cardiology unit and the ICU of Rikshospitalet in Oslo, Norway, without whom I wouldn't be alive, much less walking or writing: my eternal, inadequate thanks. The people I've met through Voksne med Medfødt Hjertefeil, a support and advocacy group for adult congenital heart defect survivors here in Norway – *hjertelig takk.*

Miriam, I could never have done this without you. I owe you everything.

# Other Routes, Further Walks

Baume, Sara, *handiwork*, Tramp Press 2020.

Beaumont, Matthew, *Nightwalking*, Verso Books 2015.

Burnett, Elizabeth-Jane, *Swims*, Penned in the Margins 2017.

Finlay, Alec, *Gathering*, Hauser & Wirth 2018.

Gleeson, Sinéad, *Constellations*, Picador 2019.

Gros, Frédéric, *A Philosophy of Walking*, Verso Books 2015.

Kagge, Erling, *Walking: One Step at a Time*, Viking 2019.

Loose, Gerry, *The Great Book of the Woods*, Corbel Stone Press 2019.

Macfarlane, Robert, *Landmarks*, Penguin Books 2016.

Shepherd, Nan, *The Living Mountain*, Canongate 2017.

Solnit, Rebecca, *Wanderlust*, Granta 2014.

Skomsvold, Kjersti Annesdatter, *Monsterhuman*, Dalkey Archive Press 2017.

Walton, Samantha, *Everybody Needs Beauty*, Bloomsbury 2021.

A wide range of songs from the Irish and British ballad traditions have also influenced this book and some are quoted throughout. They are 'Erin Go Bragh' (p. 25), 'Rocky Road to Dublin' (p. 26), 'The Factory Girl' (p. 65), 'She Moved Through the Fair' (p. 65), and 'The Manchester Rambler', which though not quoted, is mentioned on p. 71. An excerpt included from the Henry Adams Bellows translation (1936) of stanza 17 of the Poetic Edda poem 'Völuspá' appears on p. 26. Material from the Schools' Collection of the Irish National Folklore Collection inspired parts of 'Crutch' and appear on pp. 28 and 32.

**BANSHEE**
PRESS

Banshee Press was founded by writers Laura Cassidy, Claire Hennessy and Eimear Ryan. Since 2015, *Banshee* literary journal has published twice a year. The Banshee Press publishing imprint launched in 2019. Titles include *Paris Syndrome* by Lucy Sweeney Byrne, *Gold Light Shining* by Bebe Ashley, *I Want to Know That I Will Be Okay* by Deirdre Sullivan and *In Her Jaws* by Rosamund Taylor.

WWW.BANSHEELIT.COM